LET'S INVESTIGATE
Calculators

LET'S INVESTIGATE
Calculators

By Marion Smoothey
Illustrated by Ann Baum

MARSHALL CAVENDISH
NEW YORK • LONDON • TORONTO • SYDNEY

© Marshall Cavendish Corporation 1995

Published by Marshall Cavendish Corporation
2415 Jerusalem Avenue
PO Box 587
North Bellmore
New York 11710

Series created by Graham Beehag Books

Editorial consultant: Prof. Sonia Helton
University of South Florida, St. Petersburg

Library of Congress Cataloging-in-Publication Data

Smoothey, Marion,
    Calculators / by Marion Smoothey : illustrated by Ann Baum. –
    Library ed.
      p. cm. – (Lets Investigate)
    Includes index.
    ISBN 1-85435-777-8 ISBN 1-854535-773-5 (set)
    1. Calculators – Juvenile literature. [1. Calculators.]
    I. Baum, Ann. ill. II. Title. III. Series: Smoothey, Marion, 1943-
    Lets Investigate.
    QA75.S556 1995   94-19452
    513.2'078 – dc20   CIP
                                           AC

Printed in Malaysia by Times Offset (M) SDN BHD

Contents

Introduction

6

The electronic calculator is one of the most recent tools invented to help people with math, but there have been many others. This book introduces you to some of them. It also explains how to use the basic keys of an electronic calculator. There are games you can play with your calcuclator and other activities.

This book does not explain how to use the **scientific functions** that some electronic calculators have. If your calculator has these keys, first learn how to use the basic keys by doing the activities in this book. When you are sure that you know how to use them, then read your calculator's instruction booklet for further help.

As well as a basic electronic calculator, you will need cardboard, scissors, pencil, eraser, and a ruler.

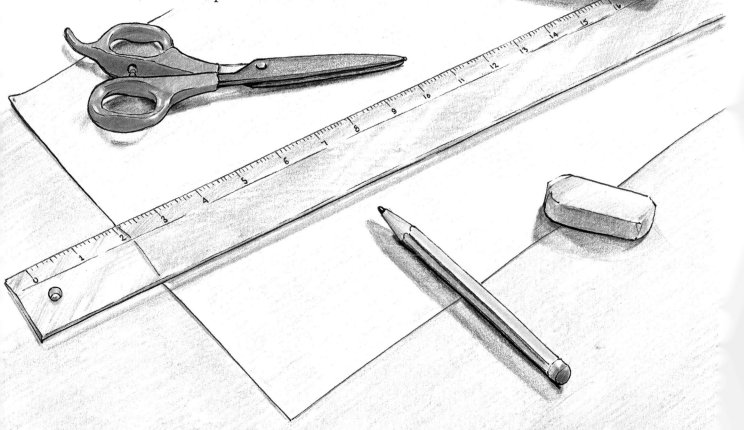

Non-electronic Calculators

Fingers and toes

People have always needed help with counting and have invented many tools to help them. Probably the earliest were fingers and toes. This may be the reason that people from most cultures count in groups of five, ten, or twenty. There are exceptions to this. The Babylonians, who lived about five thousand years ago in what is now Iraq, were skillful mathematicians who counted in sixties. Modern computers count in twos.

Tally sticks

Before recorded history, when people needed to count to more than twenty, they kept a tally by carving notches on animal bones, sticks, stones, or pieces of ivory. A wolf bone about thirty thousand years old has been found with fifty-five cuts arranged in groups of five. We still use tallying today when recording the results of a survey. Strokes for each response are grouped in fives.

The Abacus

8

The abacus is an ancient counting tool that is still in use today, particularly in Asia. In skilled hands, it is very effective.

The beads above the **horizontal** divider count as five; those below count as one.

Ready Reckoner

A ready reckoner is useful when you have to calculate varying quantities of an amount.

This section tells the cost of various numbers of items priced at 42 cents.

● **1.** How much are 49 grapefruit at 42 cents?

● **2.** In the grapefruit example, what calculation has the ready reckoner done for you?

A complete ready reckoner book has a page for each value from one cent on up. To find the cost of 120 stamps at 148 cents apiece, you first find the page for 148 cents, and then the row for 120, and read off the answer.

Sometimes you may have to find two amounts and add them together.

If you want to find out the cost of 437 stamps at 49 cents each, and the ready reckoner does not have a row for 437, you can break the calculation into two parts. Find 400 at 49 cents and 37 at 49 cents. The **sum** of the two amounts is the answer you need.

Ready Reckoner for 42¢

1	0.42	51	21.42
2	0.84	51	21.84
3	1.26	53	22.26
4	1.68	54	22.68
5	2.10	55	23.10
6	2.52	56	23.52
7	2.94	57	23.94
8	3.36	58	24.36
9	3.78	59	24.78
10	4.20	60	25.20
11	4.62	61	25.62
12	5.04	62	26.04
13	5.46	63	26.46
14	5.88	64	26.88
15	6.30	65	27.30
16	6.72	66	27.72
17	7.14	67	28.14
18	7.56	68	28.56
19	7.98	69	28.98
20	8.40	70	29.40
21	8.82	71	29.82
22	9.24	72	30.24
23	9.66	73	30.66
24	10.08	74	31.08
25	10.50	75	31.50
26	10.92	76	31.92
27	11.34	77	32.34
28	11.76	78	32.76
29	12.18	79	33.18
30	12.60	80	33.60
31	13.02	81	34.02
32	13.44	82	34.44
33	13.86	83	34.86
34	14.28	84	35.28
35	14.70	85	35.70
36	15.12	86	36.12
37	15.54	87	36.54
38	15.96	88	36.96
39	16.38	89	37.38
40	16.80	90	37.80
41	17.22	91	38.22
42	17.64	92	38.64
43	18.06	93	39.06
44	18.48	94	39.48
45	18.90	95	39.90
46	19.32	96	40.32
47	19.74	97	40.74
48	20.16	98	41.16
49	20.58	99	41.58
50	21.00	100	42.00

A Slide Rule

With the growth of the science of astronomy and improvements in engineering, people needed the answers to more complicated and precise calculations. One of the devices they used to help them was a slide rule.

The mathematician William Oughtred first thought of how to make one in the early seventeenth **century**. He was developing the earlier ideas of John Napier, who realized it was possible to turn a multiplication into a special kind of addition. These developments were taking place at the same time that Galileo was observing the movements of the moon and planets with his newly invented telescope.

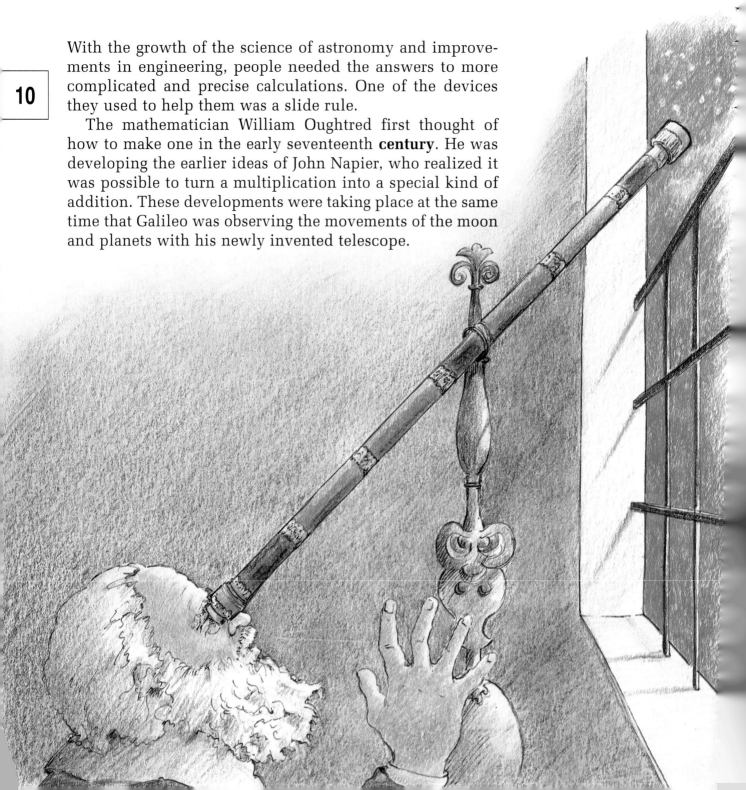

Making a simple slide rule

To make a simple slide rule for addition and subtraction, you need a piece of cardboard about 6 inches long and 3 inches wide, a pair of scissors, a pencil, and a ruler.

Draw a straight **horizontal** line across the middle of the cardboard. Mark off a scale from 0 to 9 in half-inch segments on both sides of the line.

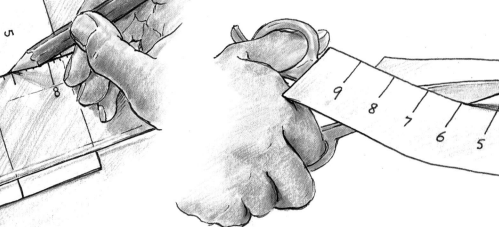

Cut carefully along the line to make two scales.

You now have a simple slide rule which you can use to add and subtract numbers.

To do the calculation 3 + 5:

1. Move the 0 of the top scale to match the 3 of the bottom scale

2. Find 5 on the top scale and read off the answer 8 from the bottom scale.

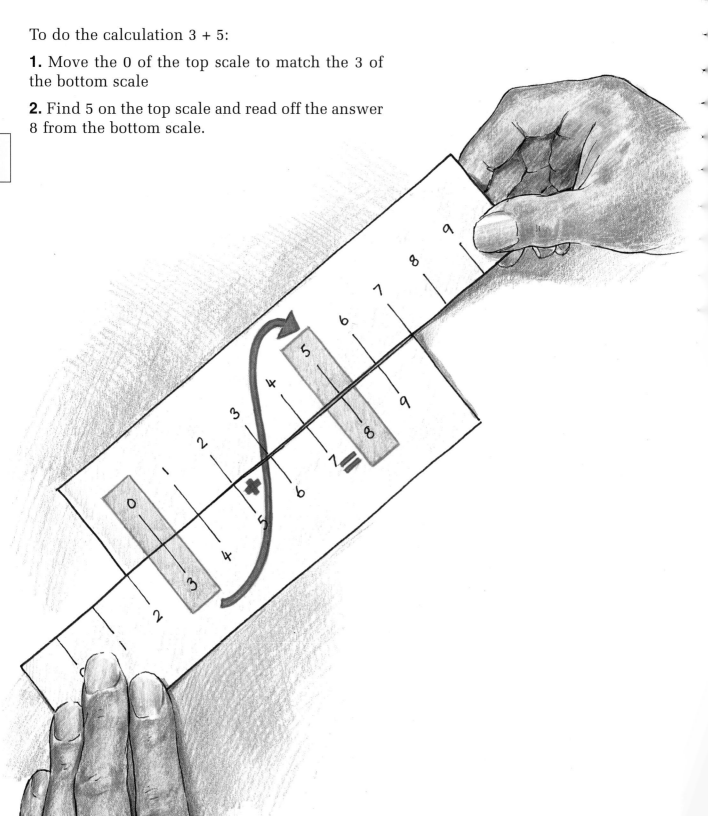

● 1. What calculation and answer does the slide rule show now?

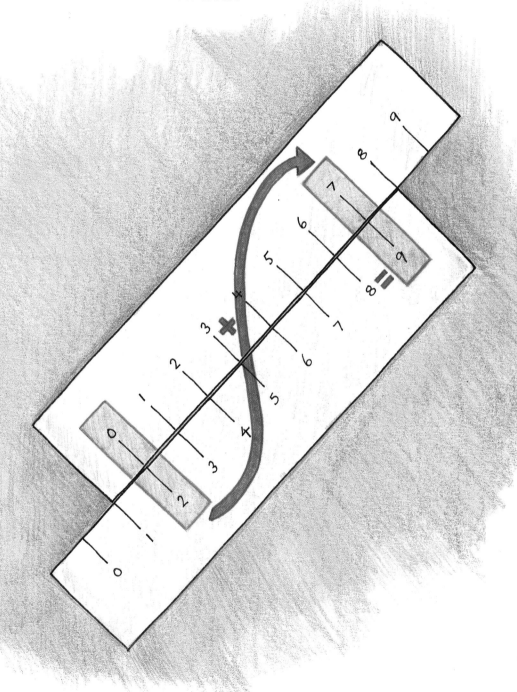

13

2. Use your slide rule to figure the answer to 9 − 4.

A slide rule that helps you to multiply and divide is even more useful.

Think about the sequence of numbers:

2 4 8 16 32 64 128

and so on.

2 is 2

4 is 2 × 2 (two 2s multiplied together)

8 is 2 × 2 × 2 (three 2s multiplied together)

32 is 2 × 2 × 2 × 2 × 2 (five 2s multiplied together)

● **1.** How many 2's do you multiply to make 16?

● **2.** What are the next two numbers in the sequence after 128?

Each of the numbers in the sequence can be made by multiplying a certain number of 2s .

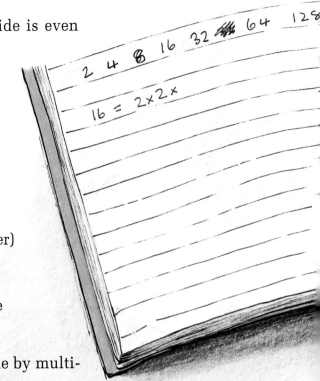

You can use this to make a slide rule for multiplication and division.

This time, one scale starts at 1 and doubles all the way along. The other scale begins at 0 and goes up in 1's. It shows the number of 2's that have to be multiplied to make the matching number on the other scale.

You can modify your addition/subtraction slide rule by adding the new scales in a different color.

15

To multiply and divide, you follow the same procedures as for addition and subtraction, but using the new scales.

This diagram shows the calculation $8 \times 32 = 256$ if you use the red numbers.

● **1.** What calculation does it show if you use the black numbers?

● **2.** Put the new scales on your slide rule and use them to figure the answers to these calculations.

(a) 16×16 **(b)** 4×128 **(c)** 32×16 **(d)** $512 \div 128$
(e) $128 \div 16$

You can see that the slide rule you have made for multiplication and division is only useful for some problems because it does not have on it all the numbers you need. You cannot use it to figure 7×39 for example.

It is possible to figure out where all the other numbers fit on the scales, but it requires more advanced math. Unlike an ordinary ruler, the numbers on a slide rule are not always evenly spaced along it.

Remember that your slide rule works for multiplication and division by calculating how many 2's are multiplied together to produce a number.

A store-bought slide rule is more complicated to use than your simple model, but it works on a similar principle.

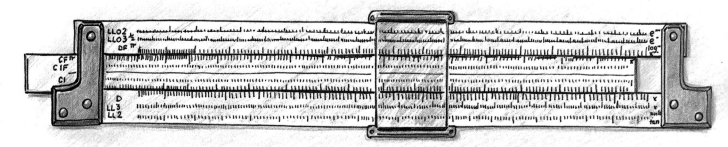

Notice that not all the numbers are evenly spaced along the scales.

Before the production of cheaply produced and portable electronic calculators, engineers used slide rules for their calculations of loads and stresses.

Napier's Rods

18

John Napier also invented another device for helping with multiplication, called Napier's rods or Napier's bones. Originally they were made of wood or bone. Make a copy on cardboard of the strips of numbers shown below and cut them out.

You can see that the set consists of an index strip of numbers from 1 to 9, a strip of zeros, and a strip for each of the multiplication tables from 1 to 9.

This diagram shows you how to use the strips to calculate 7 × 47.

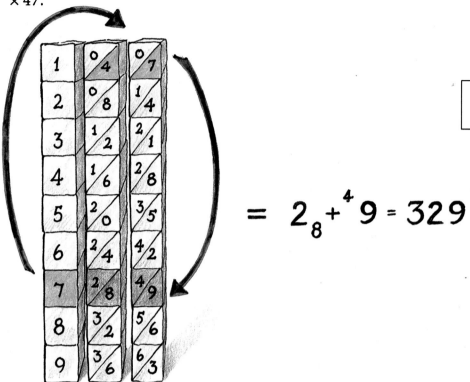

$$= 2_8 + {}^4 9 = 329$$

Notice that the middle two numbers have to be *added together* to give the number of tens in the answer. In this case, the two middle numbers are 4 and 8. 4 + 8 = 12, which means the 1 from the 12 has to be carried to the 2 in the hundreds row to make 3.

Try these examples with your cards:

● **1.** 4 × 39

● **2.** 8 × 63

● **3.** 7 × 365 (You have two sets of middle numbers to count here for the tens and for the hundreds.)

● **4.** 9 × 459 (This is a difficult one. You have to count the 8 and 5 together to make 13. Carry the 1 to the 6 and 4 for the hundreds row.)

● **5.** 23 × 501
(This is the same as 20 × 501 + 3 × 501.)

Electronic Calculators

20

During the seventeenth century, the French and German mathematicians, Pascal and Leibniz, invented calculating machines. Then in the late nineteenth century, men such as William Burroughs improved on these ideas. In 1971, Texas Instruments introduced the first pocket calculator, although it was much larger and heavier than those we use today.

Electronic pocket calculators are powered by batteries or by a cell that converts light to electricity (or is solar powered). They consist of a panel of keys and a display.

The French mathematician, Blaise Pascal, invented an early calculating machine.

Some calculators, called scientific calculators, have extra keys. We will be looking at the keys you are likely to find on a basic calculator.

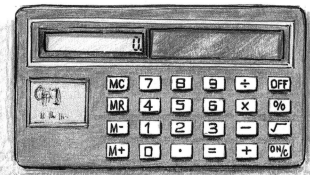

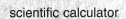
scientific calculator

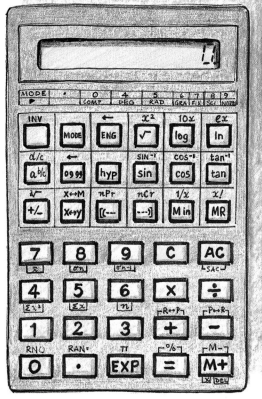

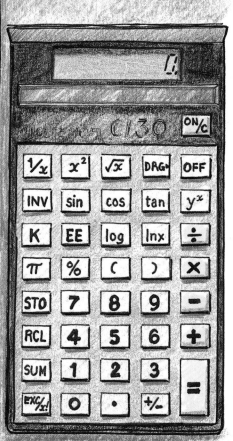
scientific calculator

Clearing the Calculator

22

Find the ON key, turn on your calculator, and look at the zero shown on the display panel. If your calculator is solar powered, it will already show 0 on the display.

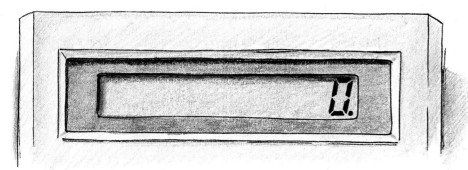

Key in the digits in order, from 1 to 9. You will need to clear your calculator after 8 because the display shows only 8 digits. There are two ways of clearing your calculator. You can clear everything you have keyed in or you can just clear the numbers in the display.

Look for a key with C on it. It may be the same key as the ON key. If you have only one key with C or CE on it, then probably pushing the key once clears only the display and pushing it twice clears the calculator completely.

If you have two keys such as CE and CA or AC, push CE once to clear the display and CA or AC once to clear everything. Turning the calculator off clears everything.

Experiment with this calculation to find how your C keys work.

- **1.** 4 + 5, press a clear key, 3 = 7 (clearing display only)
- **2.** 4 + 5, press a clear key, 3 = 3 (clearing everything)

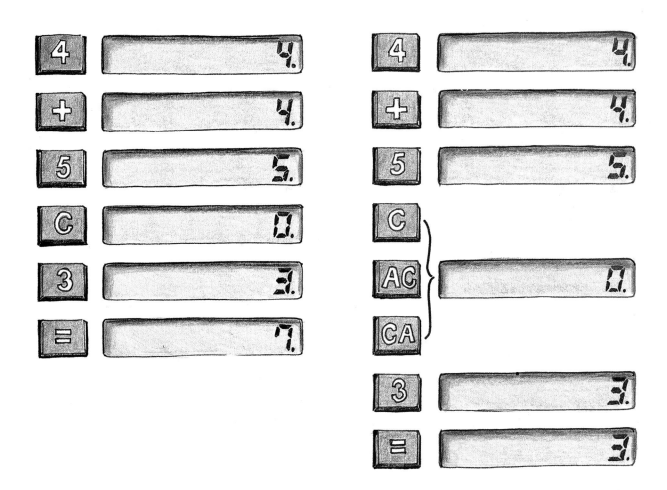

The Display

● **1.** Press the 1 key. How many segments are there in the 1 on the display?

● **2.** Investigate the number of segments in each of the other **digits** in the display.

How many sections?

● **3.** Which two digit numbers use the fewest segments?

● **4.** All the numbers in the display are based on the same shape. Which is the digit that uses all the segments of the shape?

21s – a calculator game for two

Take turns pressing the 1, 2, or 3 *and* the + keys on the same calculator. The first to show 21 in the display is the loser. Do not press the clear key between turns.

Running Totals

You found when playing 21s that your calculator will keep a *running total* while you are adding a list of numbers. You did not need to press = in order to display the sum of the numbers you added together.

● **1.** Start by keying in 21 and −. Take turns pressing 1, 2, or 3 *and* −. Does the display give you a running total?

● **2.** Start with 101 in the display and key in ×. Take turns pressing 1, 2, or 3 *and* ×. Does the display give you a running total?

● **3.** Key in 1,000 and ÷. Take turns pressing 1, 2, or 3 *and* ÷. Does the display give you a running total?

If you are adding a long list of numbers on your calculator and make a mistake, you can change the running total by clearing the display and then keep going. You do not need to clear the calculator and start again.

Try these two ways of canceling the display of a running total on your calculator.

A. 2 + 6 + 9 + 4 C 5 =

B. 2 + 6 + 9 + 4 + C + 5 =

● **4.** Which gives the correct answer for 2 + 6 + 9 ÷ 5?

You must key C before you key +, −, ×, or ÷ to cancel the last number you keyed. If you haved already keyed =, −, ×, or ÷, you will have to clear completely and begin again.

Route 166

Find a route through the numbers which adds up to 166.
Start a 3 and finish at 5.

26

Key Hopping

Look at the number keys from 1 to 9 on your calculator. They are arranged in a 3 by 3 square grid.

You can make hopping sums like this.

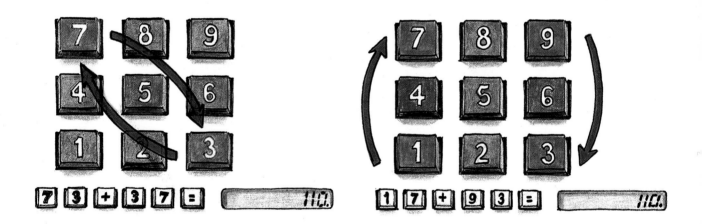

The red keys are the ones that are entered; the purple keys are hopped over.

Enter two keys, then +, then two keys.

How many ways can you find of making the sum of 110 hopping over the keys like this? You may start anywhere except at 5 and hop over one key at a time in any direction.

Getting the Answer You Want

28

Try this sum on your calculator.

$$2 + 6 \times 4 =$$

You will either get the answer 32 or 26.

If you get the answer 32, it means that your calculator works like this:

$$2 + 6 = 8; \; 8 \times 4 = 32.$$

The answer 26 means that your calculator does multiplication and division before addition and subtraction. It is figuring the sum like this:

$$6 \times 4 = 24; \; 24 + 2 = 26.$$

To make it clear which answer we want, the calculation can be written as $2 + (6 \times 4)$ which gives the answer 26 or as $(2 + 6) \times 4$ which gives the answer 32. The brackets are a signal to do that part of the calculation which is inside them first.

If there are (and) keys on your calculator, you can use them to tell your calculator which answer you want. Try keying the two sums using the bracket keys and see if you get the correct answers.

If you do not have bracket keys on your calculator, you will sometimes have to break down a calculation into separate parts by using the = key.

For example, the calculation $7 \times 3 + 12$ can mean: multiply 7 by 3 and add 12 to the **product** Written using brackets this is: $(7 \times 3) + 12$.

The calculation can also mean: add 3 to 12 and multiply the **sum** by 7.

Using brackets, this calculation is: 7 × (3 + 12).

If your calculator does not have bracket keys and does not work the way you need to get the correct answer to a calculation with brackets in it, you can overcome the problem by using the = key.

1. Key in the part of the calculation that is in brackets.

2. Key =.

3. Do not clear.

4. Key the rest of the calculation.

For example, to do the calculation 7 × (3 + 12) on a calculator that does not have bracket keys and which does multiplication first:

1. Key 3 + 12

2. Key =

3. Do not clear

4. Key × 7 =

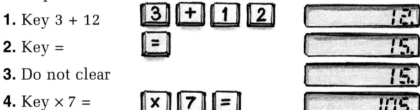

Note that you must key the × before the 7.

What are the two possible answers for each of these calculations?

- **1.** 3 × 5 + 9
- **2.** 7 − 5 × 11
- **3.** 17 × 2 − 9
- **4.** 55 ÷ 9 + 2
- **5.** 171 ÷ 3 − 7

Memory keys

You may have the keys MC or CM (clear the number in the calculator's memory), MR or RM (recall the number in the memory), M+ (add the number in the memory), and M– (subtract the number in the memory).

These keys give you another method of doing calculations with several parts that have to be done in the correct order.

Look again at the questions at the bottom of page 29.

1. $3 \times 5 + 9$

To calculate this as $(3 \times 5) + 9$, you only need to key it in.
$$3 \times 5 + 9 = 24$$

To calculate it as $3 \times (5 + 9)$, you can use memory keys.
$$5 + 9 \text{ M+} \times 3 = 42$$

2. $7 - 5 \times 11$

$(7 - 5) \times 11$ is $7 - 5$ M+ $\times$ 11 =, which gives the answer 22 in the display.

$7 - (5 \times 11)$ is 7 M+ 5 $\times$ 11 M– MR. This gives the answer –48 in the display. The – means negative 48 or 48 less than zero.

Who did it?

To find the answers to the questions, do the calculation on your calculator and turn it upside down to read the answer in the display.

If you have brackets nested inside each other, do the calculation in the inside pair of brackets first. Use memory keys if you find it helpful.

● **1.** Who fell downstairs?

$((193 \times 20) - 1) \times 2$

This means:

> multiply 193 by 20;
> subtract 1 from the **product**;
> multiply the **difference** by 2.

If you do not have bracket keys, you can use the = key and do the calculation like this:

1. 193×20
2. =
3. -1
4. =
5. $\times 2$
6. =

2. Who missed the bus?

$((597 + 5{,}157) \times 5) + 3{,}003$

This means:

add 597 and 5,157,
multiply the **sum** by 5,
add 3,003 to the **product** that results.

3. Who ate five sausages for breakfast?

$(53 + 29{,}432) \div 5 + 311{,}640$

● **4.** Who won the poetry prize?

$((1,000 \div 5) + 2) \times 4$

● **5.** Who carved the Halloween pumpkin?

$(3 \times 94 \times 7) + (4,709 \div 17) + 2,856$

Try some questions and answers of your own.

SOIL, BILE, SOB, BOILS and SOLO are just some of the possible words you can use.

Calculator Hangman

34

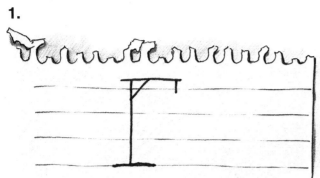

1.

You can play a number version of hangman with your friends. Instead of a word, think of an equation. For example: 39 + 78 = 117 or 702 ÷ 6 = 117.

Write this as: _ _ _ _ _ = _ _ _ and draw a gallows (1.).

2.

The rest of the players take turns to guess a number or **operation**. If the number or operation appears in the equation, enter it in the correct position. If it appears more than once, put it in each correct position. If it does not appear, draw a head (2.).

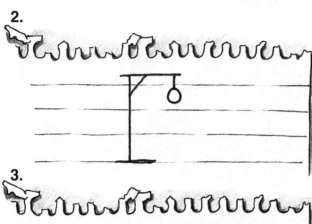

3.

The game continues until either the other players have guessed your equation or you have drawn a complete body (3.).

You may use a calculator to help you make up the equation, and the other players may use it to check their ideas before suggesting a number or operation.

If this is too easy, you can make the game more difficult by using a longer equation.

Reverso

Key in 34 × 86 = on your calculator. Write down the answer.

Reverse the **digits** of each pair so that now you key in 43 × 68 = .

● What do you notice?

● Try to find other pairs of two digit numbers that work like this when they are multiplied.

● Try to make some rules about which number pairs will work.

Challenge

The result of dividing one two-digit number by another two-digit number is 0.2125. What are the two numbers?

☆ Hints

Is the second number greater or less than the first?

What do you notice about 25 ÷ 100 and 125 ÷ 500 and 625 ÷ 2500?

Pinball

List the pins you need to hit to score 166. The ball may hit a pin more than once

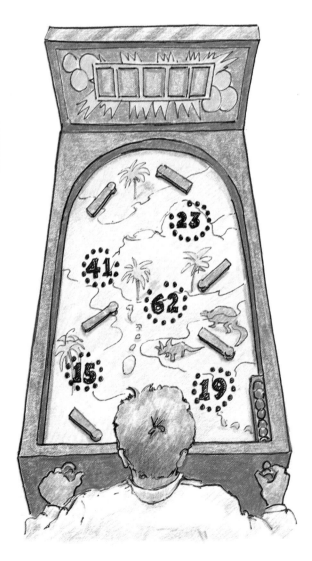

Solo Digit

Try to make the numbers from 1 to 20 using only one **digit.** Choose any one digit key that you wish. You may use the digit key as often as you need and any other keys. Use as few key strokes as possible.

You may find it helpful to use the memory keys.

Some examples:

To make the number 7 with the digit key 2:

$(2 \times 2) + 2 + (2 \div 2) =$ fourteen key strokes

or

$22 \div 2 = - 2 - 2 =$ ten key strokes

To make the number 15 with the digit key 8:

$8 - (8 \div 8) + 8 =$ ten key strokes

or, on some calculators:

$8 - 8 \div 8 + 8 =$ eight key strokes

or

$(8 + 8 + 8) \div 8 + (8 \div 8) + (88 \div 8) =$
twenty-three key strokes

Challenge

Make the number 20 in six key strokes using only 5, +, −, ×, ÷, or = keys.

Money with a Calculator

To use your calculator to figure out dollar amounts, you must use the . key. The digits before the . are dollars, and those after the . are cents.

This is the same way you write dollar amounts when you use a $ sign. $3.50 is keyed in as 3 . 50 or just 3 . 5. A zero at the *end* of figures after a . makes no difference to the amount.

A zero that is *not* at the end of figures after a decimal point is important.

3.05 means $3.05 (three dollars and five cents)

3.5 means $3.50 (three dollars fifty cents)

● Match the displays to the amounts.

● Use your calculator to figure out the cost of
these flowers and cards.

ROSES
50¢
each

RUBBER
PLANT
$50

VIOLETS
$1.09
BUNCH

Answers to page 39

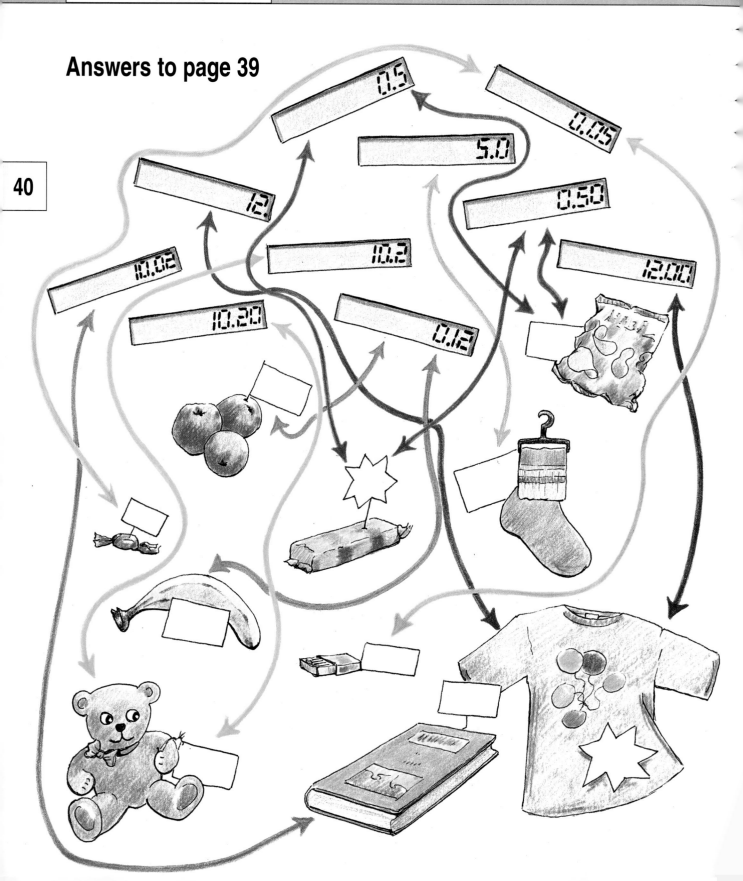

The Constant Key

You may have a key marked K on your calculator. This is called the constant key. It is useful when you need to key in a particular number repeatedly.

If you have a K key, try this: 6 + K = = =

If you get 12 then 18 followed by 24 in the display at each =, you have made the calculator use 6 as a constant and you can keep on adding 6 as long as you like by pressing =.

Now clear your calculator and try: 6 + K 5 = = =. This may give you 11, then 17, followed by 23 in the display. The constant is still 6, but the sequence begins at 5 instead of at 0.

Try changing the + first to −, next to ×, and finally to ÷ and see if the K still works.

If you have a K key and these instructions do not make it work correctly, read the instructions for your calculator.

If you do not have a K key, these are two of the ways you can try to make your calculator work like it has a K key.

Method 1

Press 6 + + 0 = = =

If the display shows 6 at the first =, 12 at the second and 18 at the third, then this has the same effect as a K key.

If you want a different starting number from the step size, try this: 6 + + 0 5 = = =

This should give you 11, 17 and 23 in the display.

Method 2

Press 0 + 6 = = = to get 6, 12, 18

Press 5 + 6 = = = to get 11, 17 and 23.

Experiment with different steps, different starting numbers, and different **operations.**

Make your calculator count down in sevens from 65 to 2.

● **1.** What happens if you keep on pressing = after 2?

42

● **2.** With 3 as the first number, what step sizes can you use to make the calculator display 52?

Wordsums

Each letter in these words has a numerical value. You are told the sum of the values of the letters in each word.

TEA = 54
LET = 47
LATE = 66
CALL = 50
TALL = 73
CULL = 35

● Figure the value of each letter so that you can give the sum of the letters in CALCULATOR.

Decimals

You have already seen from using your calculator to figure out bills that *after the decimal point* the final zeros do not matter. Your calculator probably cuts them off in the display.

Key in 5 1 . 3 0 0 0 0 =.

Look at the display. It probably shows 51.3.

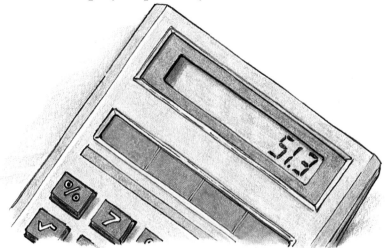

Now try 5 1. 0 3 0 0 0 =.

● **1.** What do you expect the display to show?

When you key in a decimal number, you do not need to key in the final zeros after the decimal point. Also, if you have a number like 0.1052, you do not need to key in the first zero. Your display will enter it automatically.

Key . 1 0 5 2 and watch the display.

● **2.** What key strokes do you need for this calculation?

0.025 × 10.0700

● **3.** What is the answer to the calculation?

● **4.** How can you display 0.2 using six key strokes and only the 5, +, −, ×, ÷, or = keys?

Rounding off

When you first learned to divide, you probably gave the answer 4 r 2 to the calculation 14 ÷ 3.

As you progressed and learned about decimals, you might have done something like this:

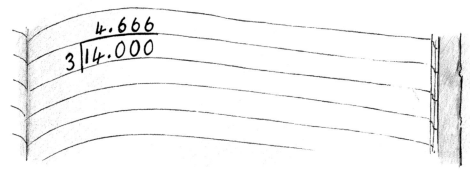

You can see that you can continue adding zeros forever, carrying the 2's and putting 6's in the answer. The answer to the calculation 14 ÷ 3 is a **recurring** decimal.

There are two ways of writing this answer.

1. You can write 4.6 as 4.6̇

2. If you are asked to give the answer to 2 decimal places, you write 4.67 because 4.666 is closer to 4.67 than it is to 4.66.

Calculators usually have spaces for eight **digits** in the display. When they have to display a recurring decimal as an answer, there are two ways they can show it.

Some calculators just display as many of the recurring digits as they have space for.

Others round off the digit in the last space.

Some decimals have a sequence of numbers that recur. Try the calculation 14 ÷ 11 in your calculator.

● **1.** What are the two numbers that recur in the decimal part of the answer in your display?

● **2.** Does your calculator round off or not?

Key the calculation 14 ÷ 13

● **3.** Some calculators display only seven figures as the answer to this. Why?

Finding Remainders

46

Wilma won a prize of $ 25,000 in a lottery. She decided to divide it equally between her six grandchildren. She figured with her calculator how much that was for each grandchild.

$25,000 \div 6 = 4,166.6666$

● **1.** Does Wilma's calculator round off?

25,000 does not divide exactly into 6. It leaves a recurring decimal. You can use your calculator to figure out how much remains if Wilma gives each grandchild $4,166.

A. Multiply the whole number part of the answer by the *divisor.*

$4,166 \times 6 = 24,996$

B. Subtract the answer from **A** from the original amount that was divided.

$25,000 - 24,996 = 4$

If Wilma gives each of her grandchildren $4,166, she will have $4 left for herself.

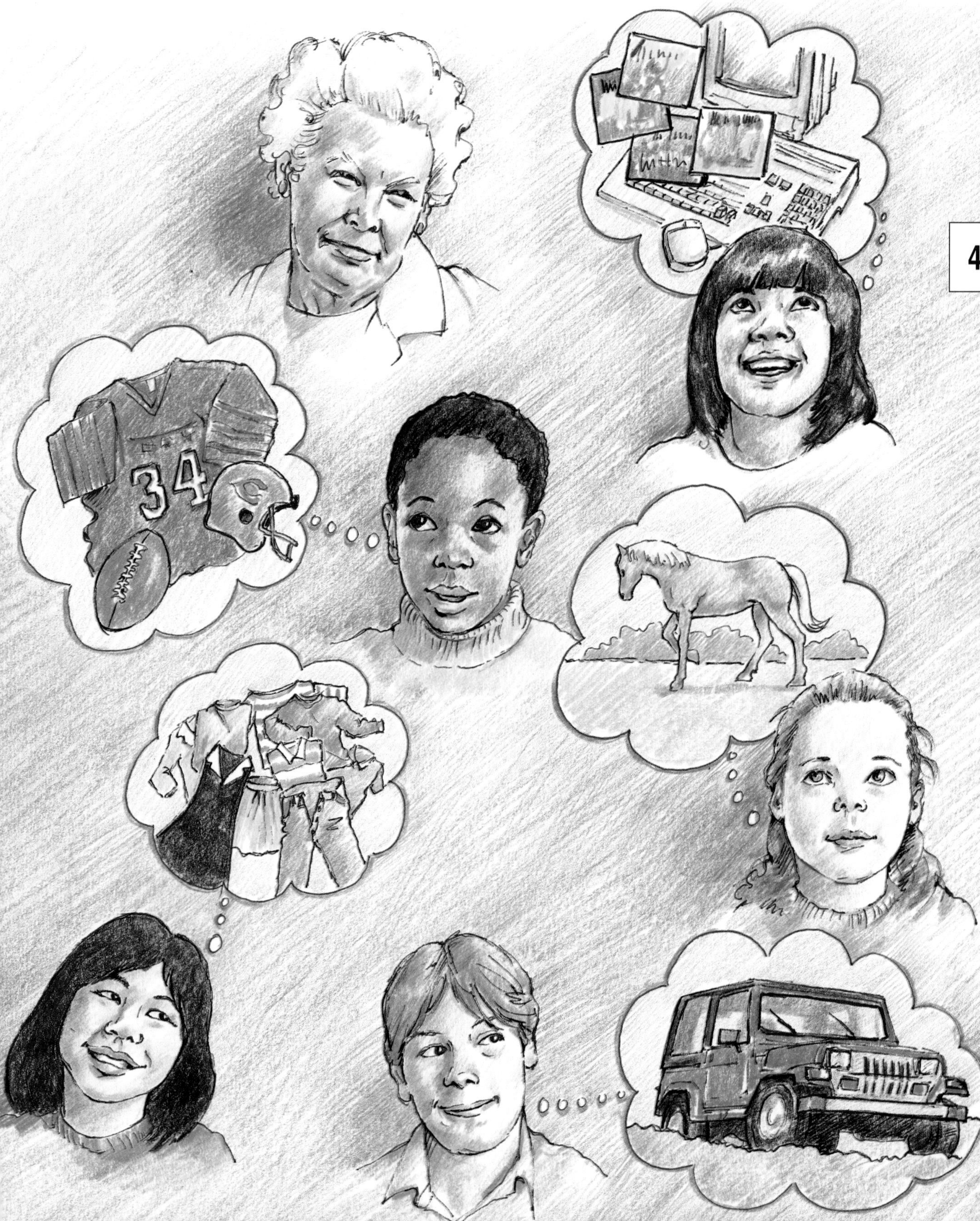
34

You can use the memory key to work out remainders.

25,000 6 = 4166.6666

4166 × 6 = 24996 M+ 25000 − MR = 4

Wayne's Mom has lent him $200 to buy a compact disc player. Wayne is going to pay it back over a year. He uses his calculator to figure how much he needs to pay.

48

The display shows $16.666666

Wayne decides to pay each month only the amount of the whole dollars in the display and to pay off the remainder at the end.

● **1.** How much must he pay each month?

● **2.** How much will Wayne still need to pay his Mom after the twelfth payment?

Xavier has 200 cakes to pack into boxes of 6.

● **1.** How many boxes does he need?

● **2.** How many cakes will be left over?

Rosalie sews on buttons and earns 80 cents for each completed garment. This style of jacket has seven buttons.

● **3.** How many jackets can Rosalie complete with 3000 buttons?

● **4.** How many buttons will be left over?

● **5.** How much will Rosalie earn?

Reminder

● **6.** How do you key 80 cents?

Multiplying Decimals

50

Use your calculator to find these **products**. Write down each calculation and answer on paper.

62×0.3
0.8×0.6
4.2×0.7
3.3×7.9
0.02×0.83
17×4.7
15.3×109
5.11×7.63
0.72×0.9
0.026×0.0003

For each answer, look at the number of **digits** after the decimal point.

● **1.** Suggest a rule for the position of the decimal point in a **product** of numbers with decimals.

Check your rule on page 62.

Now try these:

3.34×0.25
236×0.85
3.60×0.30

● **2.** The rule does not seem to be working. Explain what is happening.

It may seem strange that the product of two decimals is smaller than either of them.

Think of it like this. The calculation $0.5 \times 0.25 = ?$ can stand for, "How much is half of a quarter of an apple?"

0.5 is the same as $\frac{1}{2}$ $(1 \div 2)$ and 0.25 is the same as $\frac{1}{4}$ $(1 \div 4)$. Try them on your calculator.

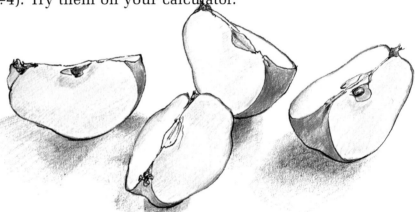

It is easy to see that the answer is one eighth.

One eighth means $1 \div 8$. The apple is divided into eight equal pieces. The decimal equivalent of one eighth is 0.125. Try $1 \div 8$ on your calculator.

Now try 0.5×0.25 on your calculator.

Fractions

To use your calculator for fractions, you have to change the fractions to decimals unless your calculator has a fraction key.

This is easy to do. You just have to remember that the line in a fraction stands for ÷.

³⁄₈ means 3 ÷ 8, which is:

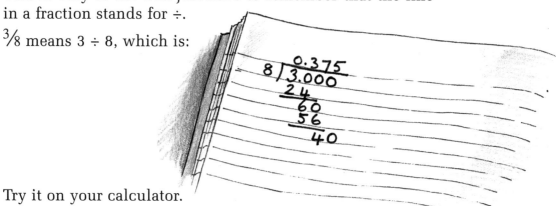

Try it on your calculator.

⁵⁄₁₀ means 5 ÷ 10.

If there are 5 candy bars to share between 10 children, how much does each child get?

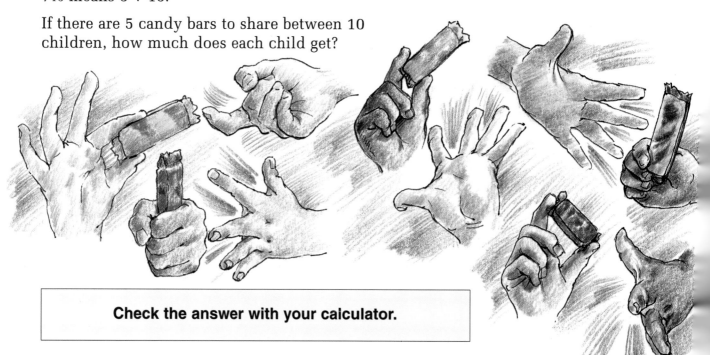

Check the answer with your calculator.

Use your calculator to find the decimal equivalents of these fractions.

- **1.** $\frac{3}{5}$
- **2.** $\frac{5}{8}$
- **3.** $\frac{7}{100}$
- **4.** $\frac{66}{88}$
- **5.** $\frac{12}{20}$
- **6.** $\frac{12}{200}$
- **7.** $\frac{12}{2000}$
- **8.** $\frac{3}{7}$
- **9.** $\frac{24}{12}$
- **10.** $\frac{9}{27}$

When you have a **mixed number** like $5\frac{1}{4}$, figure the fraction part first and then add the whole number part.

Key it in like this: $1 \div 4 = 0.25 + 5 = 5.25$

Use your calculator to help you to write these mixed numbers as decimals.

- **11.** $8\frac{1}{12}$
- **12.** $3\frac{3}{4}$
- **13.** $17\frac{3}{5}$
- **14.** $10\frac{1}{3}$

(Do you remember how to write a recurring decimal? See page 46.)

- **15.** $112\frac{53}{60}$

Very Large and Very Small Numbers

54

Try this calculation on your calculator:

11,111,111 × 11,111,111

Your calculator will give you some kind of message in the display to show that the answer has too many digits to fit into the display. The calculator is able to figure the answer but not to display it in the usual way.

You may have a display like this:

(A) 1.2346 14

or this:

(B) 1,234,567.8 E

If you figure the product with pencil and paper, you get:

$$
\begin{array}{r}
11{,}111{,}111 \times \\
11{,}111{,}111 \\
\hline
111{,}111{,}110{,}000{,}000 \\
11{,}111{,}111{,}000{,}000 \\
1{,}111{,}111{,}100{,}000 \\
111{,}111{,}110{,}000 \\
11{,}111{,}111{,}000 \\
1{,}111{,}111{,}100 \\
111{,}111{,}110 \\
11{,}111{,}111 \\
\hline
123{,}456{,}787{,}654{,}321
\end{array}
$$

If you replace all except the first digit with zeros, you get 100,000,000,000,000 or 100 trillion.

In example **(A)**, the number to the right of the display panel is telling you the size of the answer. It tells you the number of places that you need to move the decimal point to the right. Add on zeros as necessary.

The number becomes

123,460,000,000,000

The decimal point has moved to the end of the number but is not shown.

● **1.** Why does the display show 6 and not 5 as the fifth number from the left?

In example **(B)**, where the display shows 1234567.8 E, the E is warning you that the there are too many digits for the display. The number of digits *before* the decimal point tells you how many zeros to add to the right side to get the correct answer.

There are seven digits *before* the decimal point. So *remove* the decimal point and add another seven zeros.

The answer is 123,456,780,000,000.

● **2.** Does this calculator round off?

If the answer recurs, you can write the recurring numbers instead of zeros.

12,345,678 + 98,765,432 = 1.1111 08 or 1.1111111 E. You can write this as 111,110,000 or 111,111,111.

● **3.** Use your calculator for these problems. Write out the answer in ordinary numbers on paper.

(a) 22,222,222 × 101 **(b)** 12,345,678 + 98,989,898
(c) 154 × 70,707,070 **(d)** 44,444,444 + 66,666,667

If the number is very small, the number on the right of the display that tells you the size of the answer will be negative.

$0.000007 \times 0.00003 = 2.1 -10$

You have already found when multiplying decimals that the answer has as many digits to the right of the decimal point as there are in the numbers that are multiplied.

In this case, there have to be 11 digits after the decimal point. (6 in the first number and 5 in the second.) This means we must put nine zeros and the 2 and the 1 *before* the decimal point. This has the effect of moving the decimal point ten places to the left. This is why the number in the display is –10. It tells you how many places to the left you need to move the decimal point, putting in as many zeros as are required.

Finding Hidden Numbers

Some calculators hide part of an answer.

Try this on your calculator: $8\frac{4}{7} - 3\frac{2}{3}$.

Key in 8 + 4 ÷ 7 - 3 - 2 ÷ 3 =. Do not clear.

You will get 4.9047619 in the display, but the calculator has actually figured three more decimal places. You can find them by keying in − 4.9047610 × 10,000,000 = 9.048 (or 9.047 if your calculator does not round off).

048 are the hidden numbers. The calculator has figured the answer 4.09047619048.

Wipeout

A game for two players with one calculator.

Player 1 keys in a number in which all the digits are different, like 96504, and specifies which digit is to be wiped out. You wipeout a figure by replacing it with a zero.

Player 2 has to remove the digit in one turn using the − and numeric keys. For example, to wipeout the 6 in 96504, press − 6000.

Take turns keying in the starting number, and score one point each time your opponent fails to wipeout.

Now try it with decimals.

Estimating and Checking

58

An electronic calculator can be a great help when you have to figure out difficult calculations, but you have to use it sensibly. It is easy to press a wrong key and get the wrong answer. You need to have a rough idea of the answer as a check.

One method is to replace all the digits except the first of each number with zeros.

$$
\begin{array}{rcl}
37{,}593\ + & \text{becomes} & 30{,}000\ + \\
485 & & 400 \\
\underline{19{,}003} & & \underline{10{,}000} \\
57{,}081 & & 40{,}400
\end{array}
$$

The **estimate** tells you that the answer has at least six numbers in it. The answer will be more than 40,400 because you made each of the original numbers smaller in your quick check calculation.

● **1.** Estimate the answers to these calculations by replacing digits with zeros.

(a) 739×216 **(b)** $51{,}384 - 2{,}603$ **(c)** $10{,}057 + 984 - 78$
(d) $309{,}814 \div 17$ **(e)** 25.4×0.37

Another way of checking addition is to add the figures in a different order.

$37{,}593 + 485 + 19{,}003$ can be checked as $19{,}003 + 37{,}593 + 485$

To check subtraction, add the second figure to the answer and you get the first figure.

$2{,}751 - 1{,}098 = 1{,}653$

Check $1{,}653 + 1{,}098 = 2{,}751$

To check multiplication, divide the answer by one of the figures and you get the other one.

$753 \times 29 = 21{,}837$

Check $21{,}837 \div 29 = 753$ or $21{,}837 \div 1{,}753 = 29$

● **1.** How can you check this division?

$197{,}904 \div 217 = 912$

If the calculation is made up of several steps, you have to think about the answer to each step.

If you have to figure:

$(512 + 913) \times (893 - 376),$

you can estimate the answer in steps like this:

$(500 + 900) \times (800 - 300)$

$= 1{,}400 \times 500$

$= 700{,}000$

● **2.** Will the actual answer be larger or smaller than this estimate?

Your electronic calculator, like every other counting machine, is only as good as its operator. Use it wisely as a tool and you will find it a great help in your math, but don't forget that you have a very good calculator in your head as well.

Glossary

century a period of one hundred years

difference the result of subtracting one number from another

digit a finger or toe; a number from 0 to 9

divisor in a division problem, the divisor is the number of parts into which another number is divided

estimate simplified calculation to give an approximate answer

horizontal at right angles to an upright or vertical line. The horizon appears to be a horizontal straight line. (It is actually curved because the surface of the Earth is curved.)

mixed number a number that has an integer (whole number) and a fraction of a part

operation the mathematical operations in this book are addition, subtraction, multiplication, and division

product the result of multiplying numbers

scientific function keys on a calculator that carry out more complicated calculations than are frequently used in daily life

sum the result of adding numbers

Answers

Pages 8 and 9
1. $20.58
2. 49 × $0.42

Page 13
1. 2 + 7 = 9

Pages 14 and 15
1. You multiply 4 2's together to make 16.
2. The next two numbers in the sequence are 256 and 512.

Pages 16 and 17
1. 3 + 5 = 8
2. a) 256 **b)** 512 **c)** 512 **d)** 4 **e)** 8

Pages 18 and 19
1. 156
2. 504
3. 2555
4. 4131
5. 11523

Page 24
1. 2 sections
2. Digit 0 1 2 3 4 5 6 7 8 9
Sections 6 2 5 5 4 5 6 4 7 6
3. 14, 41, 17, 71
4. 8

Page 25
1. Yes
2. Yes
3. Yes

4. Method **A** gives the correct answer, which is 22.

Page 26
Route 166 – see page 63

Page 27
79 + 31, 13 + 97, 71 + 39,
73 + 37, 64 + 46, 82 + 28,
91 + 19, 17 + 93
(You can also turn all these sums round. For example, 79 + 31 and 31 + 79)

Page 29
1. 24 and 42
2. –48 and 22
3. 25 and –119
4. 8.1111111 and 5
5. 50 and –42.5

Pages 31 and 33
1. BILL
2. ELLIE
3. LESLIE
4. BOB
5. LOIS

Page 35
There are three sorts of pairs that will work.
1. Pairs of digits: for example, 33 × 66
2. Tens and units reversed: for example, 36 × 63
3. The product of the tens = the product of the units: for example, 34 × 86
(3 × 8 = 24 and 4 × 6 = 24)
Challenge
The numbers are 17 and 80.
Pinball – see page 63

Page 36
Challenge
$5 \times 5 - 5 =$

Page 37
See page 40

Pages 38 and 39
1. $2.89 (2.89)
2. $50.30 (50.3 or 50.30)
3. $8.80 (8.8 or 8.80)
4. $12.78 (12.78)
5. $1.80 (1.8 or 1.80)

Page 42
1. You get negative numbers counting down in sevens.
2. 1, 7, 0.5, 0.2, 0.1, 0.25 are a few of the possibilities.

Wordsums
C A L C U L A T E
$7 + 19 + 12 + 7 + 4 + 12 + 19 + 30 + 5 = 115$

Page 43
1. 51.03
2. $.025 \times 10.07$
3. 0.25175
4. $5 \div 5 \div 5 =$

Page 45
1. 2 and 7
2. If the last number is 3, your calculator has rounded up. If the last number is 2, your calculator has not rounded up.
3. The recurring sequence is 076923076923, and so on.
The eighth digit in the display is 0.

A calculator that does not round off just cuts off the final zero as unnecessary.
A calculator that rounds off looks at the next number, which is 7, and rounds up the zero to 1.

Pages 46 and 47
1. Yes

Page 48
1. $16
2. $8

Page 49
1. 33
2. 2
3. 428
4. 4
5. $342.40
6. .8

Page 50
1. The number of digits after the decimal point in the product is equal to the sum of the digits after the decimal point in the numbers being multiplied.
2. The calculator display is not showing the final zero(s) because they do not affect the size of the number.

Page 53
1. 0.6
2. 0.625
3. 0.07
4. 0.75
5. 0.6
6. 0.06
7. 0.006

8. 0.4285714
9. 2
10. 0.$\dot{3}$, or .3333333
11. 8.083
12. 3.75
13. 17.6
14. 10.$\dot{3}$
15. 112.883

Page 55
1. The calculator is rounding off.
2. No
3. (a) 2,244,444,444, or E 22.444444
(b) 111,340,000, or E 1.1133557
(c) 1,088,888,889, or E 108.88888
(d) 111,111,111, or E 1.1111111

Page 58
(a) $700 \times 200 = 140,000$
(b) $50,000 - 2,000 = 48,000$
(c) $10,000 + 900 - 70 = 10,830$
(d) $300,000 \div 10 = 30,000$
(e) $25 \times 0.3 = 7.5$

Page 59
1. $217 \times 912 = 197904$
2. Larger

Route 166

Pinball

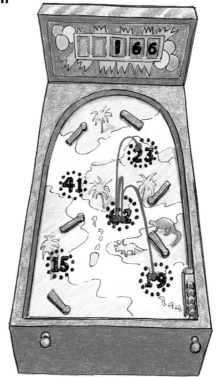

Index